10/12

1 1 MAY 2016

D1766096

Wandsworth

9030 00002 8178 6

First published in 2004 by Watling St Publishing

The Glen

Southrop

Lechlade

Gloucestershire

GL7 3NY

Printed in Italy

ISBN 1-904153-08-9

24681097531

Design: Mackerel Limited
Illustrations: Mark Davis

www.tempus-publishing.com

The Timetraveller's Guide to....

MEDIEVAL LONDON

Christine Kidney

WATLING STREET

This book is for Calum, Leah and Fergus.

CONTENTS

INTRODUCTION

When you're in Central London, in the summer, it swarms with people. It's pretty noisy, though it's mainly traffic noise that assaults your ears.

On the tube you're up close and a bit personal with your neighbour; there might be a bit of shoving to get off or on.

On the streets, perhaps on Oxford Street, you have to be very determined about where you want to go or you might get trapped behind an uncertain and dithering tourist and never meet your destination, hypnotised by their luminous rucksack. Litter spills over the bins, and on a hot day it can be pretty smelly. Vendors of slices of pizza that have seen better days catch your eye and compel you to buy some. You inch your way along the street, assailed by stacks of shoes and tracksuits and people handing you fliers advertising anything from language schools to faith healers.

It was nothing like that in the Middle Ages – in the good old medieval days.

Actually, it probably was a bit like that.

Ironically however the site of medieval London is nowadays probably the cleanest place in Central London. It's full of shiny office buildings and shiny people who work in them (except for the less shiny ones who have to escape on to the street to have a quick fag). It is the City of London with a capital C.

This isn't just because it thinks it's important – which it does – but it is where the original town Londinium was founded by the Romans. They built a wall around it, parts of which you can still see. There is even a street called London Wall which follows the direction of the wall. Places like the Oxford Street we know and love were marshy fields, with a leper colony nearby and a place of execution at Tyburn at its western end (roughly where Marble Arch is now). Westminster, where the royal court had its London home, was a village a couple of miles to the west of the city.

What we call the City (the square mile of the original town) is now the financial centre of London, of the country, and in many ways that's exactly what it was in the Middle Ages. London existed for trade and nearly everyone who lived there organized their lives around it.

CHAPTER ONE

THE STREETS

A Scratch, Sniff and Itch Guide to the Streets of Medieval London

It's hard to say what first hits you when you come through one of the gates of the city. It depends whether you've just spent the day at Smithfield meat market or whether you've just arrived from your village in Lincolnshire to try and make your fortune on the streets of London.

In the first case, it's probably a massive relief, though if you come through Newgate and down Stinking Lane, then there's only more of the same, with all those animals being slaughtered at the Shambles (also poetically known as Fleshambles) just by the Greyfriars' monastery. If you've come from the country you'd do well to bury your nose in the posy of flowers you've brought with you.

The noise is probably the first thing that hits you: shouts from water bearers, porters, wagons and church bells, the clanking from the blacksmiths' forges, stallholders selling everything from fish and spices to silk and shoes, arguments erupting between neighbours and rival tradesmen, pigs running through the streets, beggars calling for alms, animals being slaughtered, prayers from the parish churches, someone falling into a gutter and swearing inventively.

And when you've got used to the noise and the shock of the general stench, your nose might be able to distinguish certain smells particular to London – such as the breweries, slaughter houses, vinegar-makers' shops, glue-making shops, where they boil up animal bones, the burning of animal fat to make tallow for candles, the fishmongers' shops, cooking shops, the open sewers running through the streets, not to mention the odd dung heap, as well as the general household waste of the city.

Then you begin to look around you. Your village was small, a hundred people, and though you all knew each other you didn't live on top of one other. The first thing you saw when you approached the city was the giant wooden spire of the most enormous building you'd ever seen – St Paul's Cathedral.

Now you've entered the precincts of the city there are hundreds, thousands of houses packed tight together - two, even three storeys high. The top storeys jut out and in the narrower streets houses opposite each other almost touch. You can hardly see the sky. And downstairs, the house is open to the street, people are selling their goods from their front rooms – shoes, bread, fish, cloth, you name it. And they want you to buy.

By now you're hungry and your stomach has just about settled and got used to the stink of the city. You think you can get something down. There are cookshops in East Chepe and Bread Street, where if you were settled, you'd bring your own food to put in the oven there and take it back home, or there are eating houses, which are take-away shops. But you've not made your fortune yet, so you're going to make do with a meat pie and a pint from a stall and eat and drink as you go.

MEDIEVAL

ALDERSGATE

NEWGATE

LUDGATE

ST. PAUL'S
CATHEDRAL

THAMES

LAMBETHMOOR

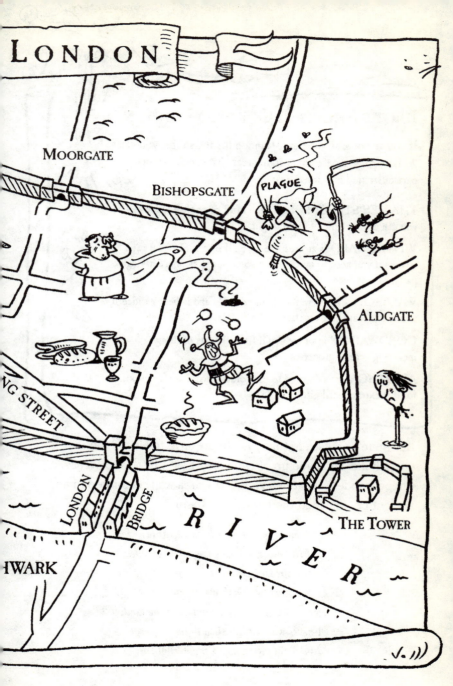

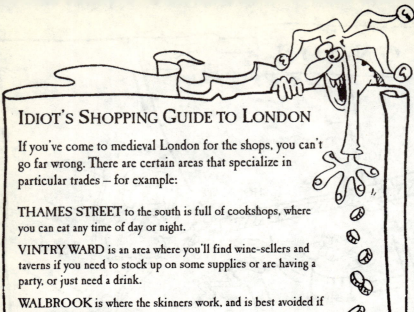

Idiot's Shopping Guide to London

If you've come to medieval London for the shops, you can't go far wrong. There are certain areas that specialize in particular trades — for example:

THAMES STREET to the south is full of cookshops, where you can eat any time of day or night.

VINTRY WARD is an area where you'll find wine-sellers and taverns if you need to stock up on some supplies or are having a party, or just need a drink.

WALBROOK is where the skinners work, and is best avoided if you're squeamish or vegetarian.

CORDWAINER is where you'll find all sorts of things, including general groceries.

ALDERSGATE is devoted to the goldsmiths, if you're looking for that extra special gift.

But there's one street that you simply have to visit if you're a shopaholic. It's made up of two parts, East Chepe and West Chepe (modern day Cheapside). The area was celebrated in an ancient poem called the London Lickpenny:

> *Then to the Chepe I began to drawe,*
> *Where mutch people I saw for to stande:*
> *One ofred me velvet, sylke, and lawne,*
> *An other he taketh me by the hande.*
> *'Here is Parys thred, the fynest in the land;'*
> *I never was used to such thyngs indeede,*
> *And wantyng money I myght not spede.*

In other words here you can get everything you want – from velvet and Paris thread to the finest silks in the land – and plenty you don't want too! You'll find vendors selling their wares either in small shops (the front room of their house) with a counter out on to the street, or if you go off the main street and into the many alleys, you will find the selds, which are mini markets, where competing stallholders will jostle for space to sell you their goods.

Off Chepe you'll find: Honey Lane, Milk Lane, Bread Street, Wood Street, Cordwainer St, Silver St, Lime St, Cannon (Candlewick) St, Roper St, Ironmonger Lane, Soper Lane, Lad (ladles) Lane, Distaff Lane, Needlers Lane, Mede Lane, Limeburner Lane, Hosier Lane.

If animals are your thing, whether you want to eat them or rescue them (though medieval Londoners would think you were bonkers to do that) you could find the beast of your choice at Cock Lane, Duck Lane, Cow Lane, Chicken Lane, Huggin Lane (for hogs) and Goose Lane. If it's animals for the table you want, then pop along to Poultry, Newgate Market, Bladder Street or Pudding Lane, where you'll find lovely meat pies and entrails.

LONDON CALLING

If you get lost on your travels, here are some useful contacts.
If you stand and shout them in the middle of one of the
Chepes, then someone is bound to know where they live and
point you in the right direction:

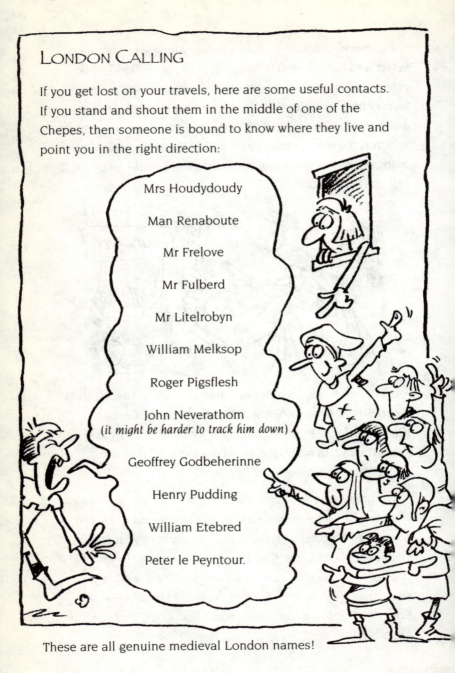

Mrs Houdydoudy

Man Renaboute

Mr Frelove

Mr Fulberd

Mr Litelrobyn

William Melksop

Roger Pigsflesh

John Neverathom
(*it might be harder to track him down*)

Geoffrey Godbeherinne

Henry Pudding

William Etebred

Peter le Peyntour.

These are all genuine medieval London names!

The thing that strikes any modern-day Londoner when contemplating a trip back to the Middle Ages has to be the drains; open sewers ran through the streets of the medieval city. All that is taken care of nowadays, away from view under our feet. But amazingly it was only organized in the last couple of hundred years. What might be even more surprising to us is that, even though they weren't very effective, there were regulations in the medieval city intended to stop the muck and flow of the city's waste.

Let's say there were 40,000 people in a square mile (that was the extent of the walled city). That's a lot of people and a lot of rotting food, poo and general waste from houses, shops and stalls, such as chicken feathers, entrails, bits of animal skins that couldn't be used... The list is quite a long one. People would chuck their waste out of their houses into the streets (woe betide any passers-by) and hope that the channels in the streets would carry the waste down to the Thames where it would magically disappear.

The area around the Fleet river, just to the west of the city wall, was quite a busy suburb of the city and there was so much dung and refuse in the river that it stopped flowing in certain places. In 1275 there was a public loo over the Fleet, which was terrible for the nearby Whitefriars monks. They complained to the then king, Edward I, that 'the putrid exhalations' from there overpowered even 'the frank-incense used in their services and had caused the death of many brethren'.

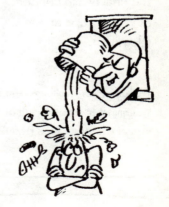

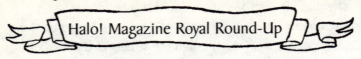
THE KING MOURNS
1290

Edward I's wife Eleanor of Castile is dead. Edward and Eleanor had sixteen children and were said to have been happily married. The Queen died near Lincoln and her body has been brought in a lengthy procession to rest finally at Westminster Abbey in London. At each resting place on her journey, a cross has been erected, the final two in London, at West Chepe and at Charing. *

(*Charing was a village west of the city on the way to Westminster. The placing of the Eleanor cross here is where we get Charing Cross from.)

The city authorities in the thirteenth century appointed 'rakers', whose job it was to clear waste away from outside people's houses pretty much like refuse collectors today. Except there weren't any nice black bin bags to keep everything neat and tidy and odour-free. If you were appointed as a raker, it was compulsory to do it. (It would have to be, wouldn't it?)

There is one tragically appropriate story about a man called Richard le Raker who went to use the privy in his house, but the wood that formed the seat was rotten and he fell down the hole and drowned in… you can imagine what.

Fines were introduced to householders:

4 pence for leaving mess outside your house

2 shillings if you leave your waste outside your house before the cart is ready to come and collect it

4 shillings if you put your waste in front of a neighbour's premises

Pigs could be a help in that they would roam about the streets, hoovering practically anything up but they could also be a bit of a menace. There you are, enjoying a quiet evening picking lice out of your loved one's hair in front of a roaring fire, when an enormous pig comes through the door and bites your leg…

Even King Edward III wrote to the mayor in 1349, the year after the plague – the dreaded Black Death – had hit London hard, complaining that the streets were 'foul with human faeces, and the air of the city poisoned to the great danger of men passing.' This was an age when they thought that the atmosphere, the air itself, had become corrupted and that this was what had started the Black Death. Edward's complaint inspired new laws and new arrangements. Four 'scavengers' per ward were responsible for clearing up the rubbish and every householder had to ensure that the area outside his house was free of waste.

Some houses, for example those over the Walbrook, paid a special tax so that they could build their toilets over the river. It became the most polluted of the city's rivers. Even London Bridge, host to 138 houses, had a public loo, which emptied its contents directly into the Thames.

Treacherous Streets

Apart from the chances of getting showered with whatever was being thrown out of a window at any point, there were other dangers facing the average medieval London pedestrian. The fact that they even named streets Dark Lane, Dirty Alley, Dirty Hill, Dirty Lane, Foul Lane and Deadman's Place gives you a wee hint that this was part of everyday life.

This was a time when you could die from a broken arm. It could get infected and there were no such things as antibiotics back then. And in the cluttered, crowded, often drunken streets of London, accidents were a regular and often fatal occurrence. You could drown in a ditch. One person 'fell into a tub of hot mash'!

Medieval London's Most Popular Fatal Accidents

You can:

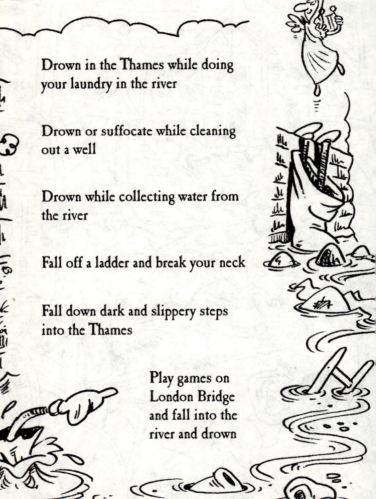

Drown in the Thames while doing your laundry in the river

Drown or suffocate while cleaning out a well

Drown while collecting water from the river

Fall off a ladder and break your neck

Fall down dark and slippery steps into the Thames

Play games on London Bridge and fall into the river and drown

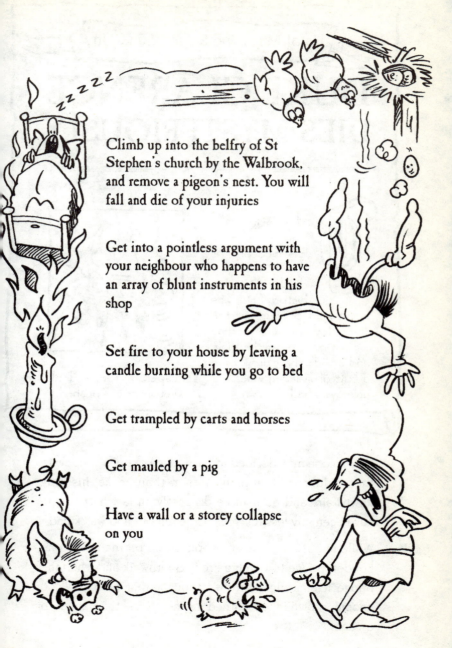

Climb up into the belfry of St Stephen's church by the Walbrook, and remove a pigeon's nest. You will fall and die of your injuries

Get into a pointless argument with your neighbour who happens to have an array of blunt instruments in his shop

Set fire to your house by leaving a candle burning while you go to bed

Get trampled by carts and horses

Get mauled by a pig

Have a wall or a storey collapse on you

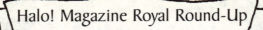
DUKE CLARENCE DIES MYSTERIOUSLY

⊹ 1478 ⊹

The brother of King Edward IV has died one of the strangest deaths in London history. He was being held prisoner at the Tower for apparent plotting against his brother the King, and is said to have drowned in a butt of malmsey wine. It is unknown whether he was

desperate for a drink or whether he was pushed.

In 1326 one man decided to have a wee out of a window in the middle of the night rather than make his way downstairs and do it more discreetly. In fact he couldn't have been any less discreet, as he fell out and was killed.

While in 1212 a crowd of people stood on the new stone London Bridge to watch a fire in Southwark and when the bridge itself caught fire, it's thought that perhaps 3000 people drowned or burned to death as they tried to escape.

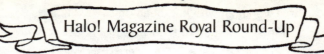
LONDON RECEPTION TURNS TO TRAGEDY
1396

King Richard II, grieving since the loss of his first wife, the loved Anne of Bohemia, brought his new nine-year-old bride, the daughter of the King of France, back to London recently to a tumultuous reception, only to see it turn quickly to tragedy after nine people were crushed in the throng.

Thank God for the night curfew! This was sounded at 9 p.m. in the summer and earlier in the winter, at dusk. First the bell of St Mary-le-Bow in Chepe rang out; then St Martin's; then St Laurence's; then St Bride's. The taverns would empty, apprentices could go home from a hard day's work, the gates of the city were locked, and the city lights – the candles and torches – were put out. All would be quiet and peaceful. The night sky in all its glory would glitter over the sleeping, resting city. Or that was the idea. It was the City authorities' attempt to save Londoners from themselves. But, surprise, surprise, it didn't always work.

In 1301 three workmen who had been on the town and missed the curfew, turned up at their master's house too late. They decided to sleep in a shed. They were discovered by the watch and were beaten so severely that one of them died.

After curfew on one night in 1322 three men lay in wait for their enemy at the corner of Soper Lane in Chepe. They attacked him and chased him toward the edge of town where he tripped over a big heap of dung, and was killed.

Again in 1322, fourteen young men came singing and shouting along Bread Street at night, way after the curfew. A shopkeeper came to his door and asked them to pipe down. They teased him and told him to come out. The shopkeeper rushed at them with a staff and knocked one of the youths on the head, killing him.

TOP TIPS FOR TIMETRAVELLERS

1. Keep your eyes up: someone may be about to empty the contents of a chamber pot over your head.
2. Keep your eyes down: you may be about to tread in some nasty substance spilling over from the open sewer running down the street.
3. Keep your eyes to the left and right: robbers abound, and are ready to take advantage of a newcomer and relieve you of your worldly goods.
4. Don't get into an argument: things escalate in this city and you might find yourself the victim of a fatal blow to the head.
5. Never wee out of a window after a few pints.

CHAPTER TWO

LONDON LIFE

HOME SWEET HOME

If you were an ordinary Londoner, the chances are you would be living in two rented rooms, maybe with a kitchen, maybe without. It might be on one floor of a building, the top floor, a solar. You would work from your house.

If you were slightly better off, a craftsman perhaps, you might live on two floors, with your shop on the ground floor, opening on to the street, where you could sell your goods. You might even own the top floor, the solar, and rent it out to someone, say a saddler, who would eventually fall out of it after having had a bit to drink.

You might own a table, two chairs, some kitchen utensils such as a frying pan and some cooking pots, some knives and spoons but no forks! (Italy and much of Europe had forks by the Middle Ages but it wasn't until 1611 when Thomas Coryat, a Tudor writer and explorer, wrote about them that the English, reluctantly, began using them.)

You might have a carpet but you've probably got rushes (straw) on the floor, sprinkled with dried herbs to take away the smells of the house, particularly if you have a cat or dog in the house.

There might be a candlestick and if you're lucky a curtain which you'll hang on the inside of your front door, to stop the draught from the street.

You can get to your upper room using a ladder, where you will have a mattress and two pillows. Your clothes might be hung on the walls, or you might have a chest to put them in. All members of the family would sleep in the same room, plus any livestock, servants or apprentices knocking about.

If you were one of the wealthier merchants, a goldsmith for example or a draper, then your house would be more lavish, although perhaps not by modern standards. You would have more space: a courtyard, a great hall, which would house a bench or two, a table, some tapestries hung on the walls to help retain the heat, a parlour, which was a bit more cosy than the great hall.

You would have valuable plate, i.e. utensils, plates and jugs to eat off and drink out of, which marked out your superior status. They might even be made of solid silver.

Your bedroom would be grander than the craftsman's but simple by today's reckoning, with little furniture. Your apprentice would sleep at the top of the house. You would still conduct your trade from your house.

Houses didn't have numbers but were called things like 'the house that recently belonged to X', which would have been very confusing if they'd had posties.

EAT, DRINK AND BE MISERABLE

One (or three) very good reasons to be miserable: preserved, pickled and dried fish. This was very big in medieval London and apparently aristocratic households bought it in bulk. Which was good news if you were a fishmonger (they were one of the better-off merchant classes) but not so good if you worked in a posh house and didn't like fish.

The staple diet of most Londoners was bread. Bakers were mostly divided into two different types: those who made 'white bread' and those who made 'tourte bread'. ('Pouffe' was French bread!) The white bread was quite fine and used in upper class or rich merchant households, whereas 'tourte' was less nice but cheaper.

Bread came from Stratford, a village outside the city. Because it was such an important part of a Londoner's diet – actually it was a staple food right across the country – it also meant that the population was very vulnerable to two things: famine when wheat crops failed and dodgy dough dealers.

The first was caused by Mother Nature, and not much could be done about that, but the City authorities – that is, the mayor and the aldermen – introduced regulations to make sure that the bakers weren't ripping off hungry Londoners. Bakers would bring their loaves by cart into town. The authorities would do spot checks to make sure that the weight of the bread was correct by weighing a random loaf. If one was found to be faulty, then the whole lot would be confiscated. In 1387 the mayor himself came to inspect the cart and one of the bakers quickly shoved a bit of iron into a loaf to increase its weight. He was discovered and the cartload was seized.

The fourteenth century was one long period of famines and plague. (It's been said that in the early 1300s when the famines were most extreme, people ate their dogs.) But when times were good, Londoners could eat well on meat, fish, eggs and

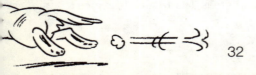

spices. The average wage of a London labourer was 6 pence a day. Here is a price list of some of the food on sale:

Meat pasty – between 5 and 8 pence

Roast goose – 7 pence

10 cooked eggs – 1 pence (a bargain if you like eggs, but think of all the people sleeping in the same room at night...).

Leg of pork – 3 pence

Meat was very popular; in later medieval London, in the fifteenth century, they ate swans, venison, partridges, root vegetables, herbs, very rich puddings with cream, sugar, almonds, dried fruits and spices.

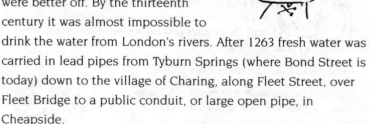

If you were thirsty you tended to reach for a drink of ale (weaker than our current beers) or wine, if you were better off. By the thirteenth century it was almost impossible to drink the water from London's rivers. After 1263 fresh water was carried in lead pipes from Tyburn Springs (where Bond Street is today) down to the village of Charing, along Fleet Street, over Fleet Bridge to a public conduit, or large open pipe, in Cheapside.

This water was free but it couldn't have been that clean – fishmongers were known to rinse their fish in it. You could pay for a private supply but, London being London, enterprising dishonest people tapped into these private supplies directing water to their own houses. While you paid, the crooks got nice, clean water for free!

HOW TO BE A DOMUS DIUS GODDESS BY LADY NYGELLA LOWSOME

Planning a Dinner Party

First of all, make sure that you have counted all your plate ware and cutlery, unless your guests are bringing their own. Freshen your hovel! Scatter some fresh herbs and dried flowers all over the floor.

Suggested Menu

Oyles Soppes (Onion and ale soup)

Take a large quantity of onions and chop them up, but not too small. Boil them for a while until soft, then drain. Heat some oil, then add the onions and a gallon of ale. Let them boil for a long time, adding saffron if you have it, and salt, adding bread at the end.

Puddyng of Purpaysse (Stuffed porpoise stomach)

Get your porpoise. Drain it of blood and fat, then mix these with oatmeal, salt, pepper and ginger, then stuff the stomach with the mixture. Simmer in water and serve.

Rysshews of fruyt (Spiced rissoles of fruit)

Soak figs and raisins in red wine, then grind them up with apples and pears which have been peeled and deseeded. Add sugar, cinnamon, cloves, mace, nutmeg and ginger. Then roll into small balls, fry in oil and serve hot.

Caudell (Ale drink)

Break six eggs and separate the yolks from the whites and place in a pot. Add several pints of ale or wine and heat gently. When the mixture starts to boil, add saffron, if you have it, salt and sugar. Serve hot.

Growing Up Is Hard To Do

There wasn't much to do as a medieval London child. It depended mainly on what sex you were and into what class you were born.

If you were a girl, you might be able to read, although you wouldn't go to school, but it was unlikely that you could write. You might get an apprenticeship as a draper or silk maker but you were really out for a husband who could look after you and whom you could help in his trade. If you were well off, the daughter of a rich merchant, you would make a good marriage with a healthy dowry. You might have children and you might survive childbirth. Or you might become a nun and go and live in a priory tending the sick and needy.

If you were a boy then there was more open to you, school for one thing. If you were the son of a freeman, you would be likely to attend an elementary school after which you would apply for an apprenticeship.

An apprenticeship could last for ten years, sometimes more, so you had to get on with whoever was training you. These were usually set up through family connections, but sometimes boys could be badly treated by their masters and there wasn't always an easy escape.

If you went to school, your teachers would be priests and most of your lessons would be in Latin. Here are some regulations from rulebooks:

NO RUNNING

NO JUMPING

NO CHATTERING

NO PLAYING

NO CARRYING OF STICKS, STONES OR BOWS

NO TRICKS UPON PASSERS-BY

NO LAUGHING OR GIGGLING IF ANYONE SINGS A HYMN BADLY

Although the Church forbade anyone to curse children, it was quite happy about beating children, even if they'd done nothing wrong – as a precaution.

A Typical Medieval Morning for a Schoolboy

- GET UP AT 5 A.M.
- HAVE A GOOD, LONG PRAY
- SPONGE AND BRUSH CLOTHES AND SHOES
- WASH HANDS AND FACE
- WASH TEETH WITH IVORY OR WOODEN STICK
- CLEAN NOSE WITH NAPKIN
- MAKE BED OR FOLD UP BEDDING IF SLEEPING ON THE FLOOR
- GREET PARENTS
- BREAKFAST: MEAT, MILK AND LIGHT BEER
- ATTEND MASS
- WALK TO SCHOOL (DO NOT TORMENT DOGS, HORSES OR HOGS ON THE WAY OR MIMIC PEOPLE BEHIND THEIR BACKS)
- DO EVERYTHING THE PRIESTS TELL YOU TO DO

GENERAL TIPS ON ETIQUETTE

- Watch where you walk and don't fall into rivers or wells
- Be careful when swimming in the Thames not to drown. Ditto when playing on London Bridge
- Boys may greet people eye to eye – girls may not
- When going to eat at somebody's house take your own knives tied to your belt
- Eat quietly. Do not scratch yourself anywhere in case people think you have fleas
- Do not pick your nose or let your nose run or touch your head
- Do not fart
- Sit up
- Do not laugh too loud

It wasn't easy being a child in medieval London. You were more vulnerable to diseases and most babies died at birth anyway. If you were of a certain social standing and became an orphan – and that could sometimes mean only your father dying, your mother could be alive and well – you could be put under the guardianship of a family friend appointed by your father before his death. Sometimes these guardians would spend your inheritance for you although the courts tried hard to protect these children.

One widowed mother, who unusually had custody of her eight-month-old daughter, tried to marry her off to the eleven-year-old son of her new husband, to keep her inheritance in the family. The baby girl was removed from her mother just in time. Forced marriages such as these were quite common and divorce almost impossible.

NINE TO FIVE

It was actually more like five to nine. And that was five in the morning to nine at night, when the curfew bells were sounded. If you were middle to upper class and didn't go on from school to become a scholar or a priest, at sixteen you would try and get an apprenticeship with one of the richer professions. All merchants belonged to a guild, which supported and regulated their members. Some were wealthier than others and there were often rivalries that could flare up into riots and even deaths between members of different guilds.

There was a premier league of merchants – the Mercers, Grocers, Drapers, Fishmongers and Goldsmiths. These were the trades that brought most money into the city, making the merchants themselves very powerful. London was split up into wards where one trade dominated and they would all appoint an alderman (a senior representative, like an MP) from whom would be chosen the mayor (a bit like the prime minister). The mayor would be the bridge between the City and the royals at Court, which most of the time must have seemed very removed from the daily life of Londoners.

How to Court at Court

If you get a chance to visit the Court, you must adopt a completely different set of rules. Young men must be pale, you must look longingly at beautiful young maidens and refuse your dinner because you are pining for them. You probably should not talk to them directly, but send them soppy poems about how much you esteem them, their virtue and their beauty, and how low you regard yourself in relation to them.

You may go hawking and participate in a bit of hunting, but don't look as if you're having too good a time. Everyone will think you are very trendy, a model of courtly behaviour, and you may well be invited back.

HERE ARE SOME OF THE RULES OF LOVE, FROM THE COURT'S HANDBOOK TO ROMANCE

1. If your beloved dies, you must mourn for two years
2. Every lover turns pale in the presence of his beloved
3. When he sees his beloved, a young man's heart beats wildly
4. A young man in love is always afraid
5. A young man in love is always pale and hardly sleeps
6. A young man in love always thinks the worst of his beloved out of jealousy
7. A young man in love always has a picture in his mind of his beloved

ALTHOUGH THIS MIGHT SOUND SOPPY TO TIMETRAVELLERS, IT IS ACTUALLY VERY HARD WORK.

An apprenticeship usually lasted ten years. There were quite a few trades or crafts you could choose from, including: pepperer (grocer), cobbler, tailor, hatter, metalworker, spectacle-maker, goldsmith, clothmaker, stonemason, innkeeper, corsour (horse-dealer), marbeler, bookbinder, jeweller, organ-maker, feathermonger, piemaker, basket-maker, mirrorer, quilter, maker of parchment, raker or barber-surgeon.

Now this last one – barber-surgeon – is quite curious. If you were ill would you go to a hairdresser? Or if you needed a new haircut would you visit the doctor? No? Of course not.

However, in the Middle Ages you would have. Back then barbers were also surgeons and surgeons were also barbers! The red and white poles outside traditional barbers' shops are a hand-down from the bloodstained rags that barber-surgeons used to hang outside their shops.

Thankfully during the later Middle Ages surgeons started concentrating on medicine and barbers on haircuts. But until very recently if you had a broken leg you were actually probably safer having a haircut than being seen by a doctor.

Ezekiel Blodspout's Chopping Shop

Cut, blow dry and boils lanced – 1 pence

Trim plus any one limb amputated – 2 pence

Cut, dry and general blood-letting – 2 pence

Dry cut and trepanning* – 2 pence

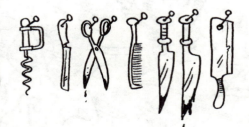

* A hole drilled in head to release 'humours' (bad spirits) in the body

FREEDOM

Once you had finished your apprenticeship, you gained your freedom of the city. This was highly valued. The apprentice would have to go before the mayor, accompanied by his employer, who would give him a good character reference and his licence to trade. This would be registered at the Guildhall.

However, if your master died before you completed your apprenticeship, you could be left to someone else in his will! You could gain your freedom in three other ways too: through birth, by buying it and by the king recommending it.

If you had the bad luck to be born in serfdom, you weren't entitled to any of the above – you couldn't even become an apprentice but would toil the rest of your life as a workman, an employee perhaps of a craftsman.

However non-citizens, from the rural villages just outside London, were allowed to sell leather, metalware, meat, hay, poultry, fish, fruit and vegetables, butter and cheese in markets held in the morning, but they had to sell everything off before the market closed!

There were also markets in the late evening, before the curfew, but when it was starting to get dark. Here Delboys of their day would sell stolen or faulty goods. These markets also tended to attract petty thieves and prostitutes.

If you were selling new clothes and cloth you had to sell them in broad daylight, so customers wouldn't be sold shoddy goods. However 'frippery' (that is, second-hand clothes, shoes and furniture) were sold in the evening markets at Cornhill and Chepe.

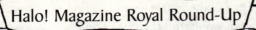
MAGNA COCK-UP

1216

Ever since Magna-Carta King John went back on his promises, rich London merchants and dukes have been trying to get rid of him. They even invited Louis, eldest son of the French King Philip II, to take the crown of England, offering him 1000 marks to come. Louis landed in England and marched to Southwark earlier this year, coming over London Bridge to St Paul's Cathedral. But since the recent death of King John, it seems that Londoners have changed their mind and have opted to crown John's son Henry as king instead, even though he is only a child. It appears that Louis is asking for 10,000 marks to go back to France.

Top Tips for Medieval Timetravellers

1. Don't whatever you do get born into serfdom
2. Don't get orphaned, particularly if your father isn't a freeman
3. Don't buy your wedding outfit in the evening
4. Don't be rude to priests
5. If you have a sore throat, don't get your hair cut

CHAPTER THREE

HOLY DAYS

Everyday life in medieval London could be a grind. It was hard work, whether you were rich or poor.

If the king was off fighting some crazy crusade or at war with the French (again), or just feeling greedy he'd raise taxes, hitting Londoners where it always hurts them most – in their purses!

There was a lot of tension – people lived on top of each other in very small areas. Arguments could easily flare into full-blown fights and as people carried knives or swords, murders were common.

FOURTEEN-YEAR-OLD KING QUELLS SAVAGE REBELLION

1381

An uprising, which we can only call a Peasants' Revolt, has miraculously dispersed after threatening to kill the King and overturn his authority. A roofer called Wat Tyler was its ringleader. It's thought that Tyler gathered 100,000 men to march on London, coming over London Bridge from Southwark and taking the City, while gaining support from many Londoners as he went. There was a lot of ruthless and random killing, particularly of foreigners. Some of the rebels beheaded these poor victims and carried their heads on sticks as they progressed through the city.

They eventually gained control of the Tower, where they seized the object of their fury – Simon of Sudbury who held both the post of Archbishop of Canterbury and Chancellor – i.e., the man who was trying to levy all the crippling taxes that sparked off the rebellion in the first place. He, along with Sir Robert Hailles, the Treasurer, were beheaded on Tower Hill. In a gruesome gesture, the rebels nailed the Archbishop's cap to his skull and marched with his head through the city. They attacked the luxurious Savoy

Palace, burning and throwing into the Thames the beautiful tapestries, jewels and clothes inside. King Richard, only fourteen years of age, agreed to meet Tyler and his followers at Smithfield. Tyler stated his

Tyler was treated at St Bartholomew's only to be fished out and finished off by another member of the royal party. Richard, thinking very fast on his young feet, promised the crowd concessions and to be their true

demands. In a turn of events that could have sent the city spiralling into chaos, William Walworth, the Mayor, thinking that Tyler had been disrespectful to the young King, stabbed him as he pulled him from his horse.

leader. Amazingly, the crowd was calmed and shuffled off relatively peacefully. Tyler's head replaced those of the Archbishop and Treasurer on London Bridge. The poll tax will be scrapped.

THE WORD ON THE STREETS

If you're destined to spend your time in medieval London on the streets, there's really no point in trying to be polite to people (although do make sure when you are rude, that your insultee is not in easy reach of a blunt instrument). Here are some phrases that will give anyone you speak to a flush on his cheeks.

Medieval Latin *(Advanced Level)*

Tu sochors! – You idiot!

Tu scibalum hedi! – You goat dung!

Tu scibalum ouis! – Sheep dung!

Tu scibalum equi! – You horse dung!

Tu fimous bouis! – You cow dung!

Tu stercus porci! – You pig filth!

Tu hominis stercus! – You human dung!

Tu canis scibalum! – You dog dung!

Tu vulpis scibalum! – You fox dung!

Tu muricipis scibalum! – You cat dung!

Tu galline stercus! – You chicken droppings!

Tu asini scibalum! – You donkey dung!

Tu vechors et semichors! – You idiot and halfwit!

Tu scurra – You buffoon!

(*Sharp students will observe that apart from the last two insults, there is a theme that runs through these phrases.*)

Death was always around the corner whether down some slippery steps to the river, whether you were innocently going about your business crossing the road, or if your auntie started having a sneezing and coughing fit while sitting next to you at the table!

So at certain times of the year there would be performances, festivals, celebrations and pageants, which meant that everyone in the city could don their party gear and let off some serious medieval steam.

GEOFFROI POINTYBERD'S
Theatre Guide to
MEDIEVAL LONDON

****Must see ***Good **OK *Poor

MYSTERY and MIRACLE PLAYS

These happen around religious festivals, usually at Easter and Christmas. They are biblical stories enacted by priests, actors, sometimes members of different guilds who fancy themselves as actors. The best one to catch is Noah's Flood. The special effects can be amazing in that one!

On the whole they are very long and very boring but at least they're in English and not Latin. You might find them in churches, but these days they are more likely to be performed in the streets, on scaffolds or even in carts that move around the city. Clerkenwell is a good place to see them. Occasionally the actors will bring in a bit of comedy, usually at the expense of the devil, who will often be spat at, hit, tripped up and generally knocked about. The best performances are by the Parish Clerks and the St Paul's boy choristers. **

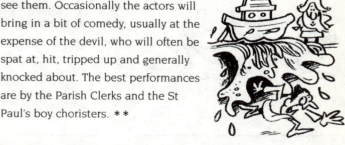

Morality Plays

These are perhaps the most boring of all the entertainments available in the city. This is all about Man and the Day of Judgement and how the Vices try and tempt him and the Virtues try and save him. The main character is usually called Everyman or something dull like that and he is a complete idiot. Try and avoid these if you can, but pressure will be put on you to attend by religious folk intent on improving your soul. *

Interludes

A must! These are usually around Shrovetide and sometimes appear with the religious plays above, or are performed on their own. They're mostly knock-about slapstick farces about sex and farting and are hugely popular. King Richard II is a fan. You might have to queue.
* * * *

Puppet Plays and Dumb Shows

If you're sick of religious spectacle, then these are for you!
The Fall of Troy, the story of Joan of Arc, fables about cheating merchants and the devil in disguise are the subjects of these. Different companies use mime acts or puppets. ***

Feasts

If you're going to see one thing in London, see these. They are performed by a special band of actors called the Fool's Company, who are an anonymous, underground group of actors who go into churches and take the mickey out of the services. They turn the church into a ballroom and the altar into a bar. You have to keep your ear to the ground as they won't advertise beforehand in case they get caught. Amazingly the Church hasn't suppressed them yet, but there would probably be riots in the streets if they tried to. ****

Street Theatre

This is readily available throughout the year, with minstrels, musicians, acrobats and – our favourite – the podicicinists, those sophisticated entertainers who can fart any tune you request. ****

The religious festivals were times when people really let their hair down and were encouraged to by the authorities. There were two main celebrations – on Midsummer Day and at Christmas.

Normally most evenings were quiet because of the curfew, but the Midsummer Day celebrations lasted late into the night. Londoners celebrated with bonfires, pageants and dancing, with musicians, giant effigies and (oh dear) morris dancing. The alderman of each ward had to appoint the most responsible citizens to form the watch – to keep order, to form part of the procession and to make sure that there weren't any major fires.

In the summer, bonfires and drink naturally made them nervous. People got up in fancy dress, wearing masks and false beards (this was normally a crime). Houses were decorated with flowers and branches and most Londoners set out tables with food and drink for their friends and those they had been quarrelling with. It was a time to kiss and mask up… sorry, make up.

At Christmas the world was turned upside down again. The Festival of the Boy Bishop was something that every schoolboy must have been desperate to take part in.

For two weeks over Christmas the cleverest boy in the school would become the Headmaster (who would normally be a senior Church figure) and his mates would become the other masters. They would then travel around to the rich houses of London, where the boy bishop would sit in the place of honour, eating the best food and boring their hosts senseless with sermons that bored the boys the other fifty weeks of the year. Nice work if you can get it.

The Lord of Misrule was also a job that you could only get over Christmas. Someone would be chosen to turn all the ordinary rules on their head, to do anything he chose, which was mainly to drink and be a bit naughty. When we pull crackers at Christmas, this is the link back to the period of misrule at Christmas, and the paper hat represents the crown that the Lord of Misrule would have worn.

Apart from these public parties, there were also lots of spectacles put on at special occasions. When Edward II's son was born, the channel that supplied fresh water in Chepe was filled with free wine!

THIS SPORTING LIFE

Jolly Jousts

Jousting was a very popular spectator sport, particularly in the reigns of Edward III and Richard II. It's a contest where two men on horseback ride at each other from a distance, pointing a big pole in front of them. The aim is to knock the other chap off his horse. Edward III was a fan of the legends of King Arthur and believed jousting would help revive an Age of Chivalry, i.e., knights with good manners who liked horse riding and poking people with big sticks.

To an average Londoner it must have looked amazing to see the knights dressed in their coloured robes, with their horses in matching outfits. These knights would be led from the Tower by chains, sometimes made of silver, sometimes of roses, by maidens who rode before them on horseback. The tournaments were held in Chepe or by London Bridge.

THE QUEEN GETS A SORE BUM

1329

Edward III's greatly anticipated jousting tournament at Chepe turned into farce today, narrowly avoiding tragedy. The streets looked spectacular – they were cleared of the usual London muck, and bunting decorated the houses. An archway was erected across the street so that Queen Phillipa and her ladies could watch. However, when they climbed up to the archway disaster struck and it collapsed in the middle. The Queen and her ladies fell on top of the knights who incredibly were passing under it just at that moment. It was a miracle that nobody was killed, although it was said that the King was about to despatch the carpenters to an early death when the Queen intervened and begged that their lives be spared. It is rumoured that the King will build a permanent structure next to Bow Church to watch the tournaments in the future. Nice things are being said about the Queen across town.

BATTLE FOR THE BALL

There were also lots of games young men could play to let their hair down. Outside the walls of the city football was played nearly every day, although it was considered very dangerous and was even banned at one point by the mayor of London (although no one took any notice).

The ball was made of a pig's bladder stuffed with dried peas and sewn up tightly. Someone not playing would throw the ball high into the air and then run for dear life as the two teams fought for possession. There was one rule: to get the ball into your opponent's goal, no matter how many people you knocked over. There are records of broken limbs, broken noses and the odd death from playing. No one was penalized.

There's no doubt that most of the games that young people played were rehearsals for battle – they were meant to toughen you up.

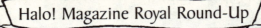
COURTLY KING PASSES AWAY

1377

The man who brought glamour to the Court, who brought the Age of Chivalry alive and gave us our cult of King Arthur, has passed away, after a long battle with senility.

The city and the nation will grieve the loss of their most royal King, a brave solider in war and a keen sportsman in peacetime. Famed for setting up the Order of the Garter, which in King Arthur-style was a group of twenty-six knights who swore to gaining the French Crown, Edward III will never be matched.

His body will be carried in an open casket through the City to Westminster Abbey, where he will be buried beside his Queen, Phillipa, who died of the plague in 1369.

Holiday On Ice

In winter, marshy land at Moorfields would freeze and people would go ice-skating. Here is a description of ice-skating in London from the twelfth century:

'Some… put on their feet the shinbones of animals binding them firmly round their ankles, and, holding poles shod with iron in their hands, which they strike from time to time against the ice, they are propelled swift as a bird in flight or a bolt shot from an engine of war.'

Wet Winner

One bizarre game – water quantain – was played at Easter. A tree was fixed in the middle of the Thames, with a target attached to it. A young man carrying a lance was rowed in a boat and was launched at the target. If he missed, he fell in the river.

Game On

Other games included tamer versions of jousting, wrestling, archery, mock river battles as well as the usual cockfighting and bear-baiting. Many of these were played at Bartholomew Fair once a year at Smithfield, just west of the city wall. This was a very famous fair, which was started by a former jester turned prior of St Bartholomew's.

He set it up in the twelfth century as a cloth fair, intended to help the priory funds. However it developed into London's most famous carnival, lively and outrageous, with jugglers, fire-eaters and tightrope walkers, and was made immortal by the Elizabethan playwright Ben Jonson. Although uptight Victorians banned it in 1855, it has recently made a comeback but it's nothing like the spectacle it once was.

OUR HERO RETURNS

⊹ 1415 ⊹

Henry V, our king – son of Henry IV, who knocked King Richard II off the throne, has returned in triumph to London after his magnificent defeat of the French at Agincourt. Londoners greeted his arrival with almost hysterical excitement. Great giants adorned the entrance to London Bridge from the south. As he progressed along the bridge, he met boys dressed as angels in white with glittering wings, garlanded with laurels.

Cornhill was covered with a canopy of crimson cloth for him to walk on and as he walked down Chepe, sparrows and other small birds were released in celebration. The king seemed to enjoy himself as a host of young girls blew golden leaves in his direction.

He is one of our most popular kings, not least because he gave the French a really good thrashing.

TOP TIPS FOR TIMETRAVELLERS

1. If someone invites you to a morality play, say you're busy
2. Get a sick note from your mum on water quantain day
3. Make a list of the people you'd most like to bore the hose off when you get made Boy Bishop
4. Don't laugh your head off when royalty falls on its bum
5. Forget the offside rule (if you ever knew it in the first place)

CHAPTER FOUR

THE MIASMIC METROPOLIS

Well, you've had just about as much fun as medieval London has to offer. Now it's time to come back to the real world.

Even at the best of times, the Middle Ages were medically and hygienically challenged. There were all sorts of unpleasant diseases knocking about, including: TB, typhus, influenza, leprosy, dysentery, smallpox, diphtheria, measles, and according to the poet William Langland, 'fevers and fluxes, coughs, heart disease, cramps, toothaches, catarrhs and cataracts, scabs, boils, tumours, burning agues, frenzies and foul evils'.

We know enough now about the causes of diseases to see that the way people lived in medieval London must have contributed to how ill they got.

But the one disease we remember most is the Black Death, or the Great Pestilence as they called it at the time, that devastating plague that swept the world and killed about a third of the population of England and its neighbours from 1348 to 1349. It kept returning over the following centuries until the last bout in 1665.

The nation had been weakened by the famines affecting the country in the early 1300s. In London in 1322 a crowd of starving poor were waiting for alms (charity) left to them in a will by a fishmonger in order to buy food. Fifty-two people were crushed to death in the rush.

These famines must have reduced the country's resistance to the disease, although plenty of well-fed people didn't escape its devastation.

The bacterium that caused the plague lived in the stomach of fleas, which found their most comfortable dwelling on the bodies of rats. These rats were well-travelled rats and came to England on the spice ships from the East, where it's thought the plague originated. There were two types of plague, though both were usually fatal.

1. The Pretty Deadly Plague

With this the victim developed buboes, nasty swellings in the groin, armpit and neck that could grow to the size of an apple or even larger. After five or six days the victim would either die or, very, very rarely, make a miraculous recovery.

2. The Really Very Deadly Plague

With this type the victim did not always develop buboes, though they usually did, but they would cough up blood. The coughing lasted two or three days and then you died. Some people died within hours after catching the disease.

As if that wasn't bad enough, the smell of the patient was unbearable. Their breath, sweat, wee etc. ('nuff said) produced an appalling stench.

Medieval doctors were split over what had caused this dreadful disease. One theory, though completely wrong, is understandable, given the disgusting conditions that we have seen on the streets of the city. This was that the air had been poisoned, creating a miasma, which people had to breathe, thus becoming infected. Here are some other wilder theories bandied about:

It was caused by:

1. Planetary movement
2. Extreme weather changes
3. Someone had broken a phial containing poison when the wind was blowing in the direction of a city he wanted to infect, the disease then spread from here
4. Earthquakes emitting poisonous fumes into the atmosphere
5. A look from an infected person releasing an 'aerial spirit' from their eyeball

Although no one could come up with any cures, there were also theories about how to prevent catching the plague:

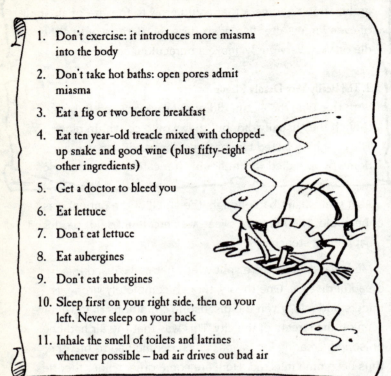

1. Don't exercise: it introduces more miasma into the body

2. Don't take hot baths: open pores admit miasma

3. Eat a fig or two before breakfast

4. Eat ten year-old treacle mixed with chopped-up snake and good wine (plus fifty-eight other ingredients)

5. Get a doctor to bleed you

6. Eat lettuce

7. Don't eat lettuce

8. Eat aubergines

9. Don't eat aubergines

10. Sleep first on your right side, then on your left. Never sleep on your back

11. Inhale the smell of toilets and latrines whenever possible – bad air drives out bad air

In 1348 before the plague, the population of London is thought to have been about 50,000–60,000. Between 20,000 and 30,000 people had died by 1349.

There were so many deaths that the existing graveyards couldn't cope with the numbers. Two new cemeteries were opened near Smithfield.

A mass grave south of the Thames at Southwark was opened where it was said that at the plague's height two hundred bodies were buried every day. There were so many deaths that we don't have many records of who they all were, but we do know that there was a big grave for the monks who died at Westminster Abbey and about one hundred Greyfriars fell victim. Even royalty weren't immune. Though it was during a later bout, Phillipa, the nice queen who fell on the knights at the jousting tournament at Chepe, succumbed to the disease in 1369.

WHICH DOCTOR?

There were three types of healers in the Middle Ages: the university-trained physicians, monks who tended the sick, and wise women out in the villages. All of them used the same cures made from plants and herbs. But these wise women eventually became the victims of witch-hunts in later centuries – probably because their cures were more successful! You chose your healer depending on how rich you were, with the physicians tending the very wealthy.

Medieval doctors believed that all human bodies were made up of four humours and that all illnesses were caused by an imbalance of these due to outside influences. The medicine given was meant to rebalance these humours and heal the patient. The four humours were:

1. **Sanguine** (blood), which was hot and moist
2. **Choler**, which was hot and dry
3. **Phlegm**, which was cold and moist
4. **Melancholy**, which was cold and dry
   (Top tip: don't try too hard to understand this – life is too short. But not as short as it was then, thankfully.)

Can you match the cures with the disease?

1. Place buttercups in a bag and hang round neck
2. Rub goose droppings over your head
3. Touch a dead man's tooth
4. Tie an eel skin around your knee

A) Cures baldness
B) Cures toothache
C) Alleviate cramps
D) Cures insanity

Answers 1D, 2A, 3B, 4C

Most of the sick in London weren't cured at all – they thought it was more important to call a priest than a doctor and, let's face it, it was probably just about as useful. But the Church played a big part in people's lives, not least in setting up hospitals where they would look after the dying and the poor.

TOP TIPS FOR TIMETRAVELLERS

1. Try not to go bald unless you like goose droppings smeared on your head
2. If someone gives you a pet rat circa 1348, politely refuse the gift and emigrate
3. Holidays in China and India in the early 1300s are not recommended
4. If you're journeying back to London in the early 1300s make sure you pack plenty of extra sandwiches
5. Take a modern doctor with you

CHAPTER FIVE

HOLY SMOKE

Medieval London was a place of superstition and fear. As we've seen, life was hard and often very short. The Church was very important in people's lives – sometimes stoking up that fear and superstition, sometimes genuinely helping those in need.

Like all things in medieval London life, the Church was a creature of extremes. For example, if you had leprosy, you would be taken care of at the hospital at St Giles-in-the-Fields (near modern-day Centrepoint around Tottenham Court Road tube station) but if you died and it was thought you had committed suicide, your body would be thrown over the city wall to moulder in a ditch somewhere. And just as some holy folk were decent, honest and hardworking, some were not.

There were all sorts of jobs you could get in the Church – you could be a parish priest, friar, abbot, summoner, pardoner, a parson, an abbess, a nun, a prior. And we get a pretty good picture of them from one of our greatest writers, the Londoner Geoffrey Chaucer, who wrote a poem called *The Canterbury Tales*.

THE CULT OF THE SAINTS

There was a very strange craze that swept medieval Europe in the early Middle Ages – it was the worship of bits and pieces belonging to dead saints, whether old garments or their old bones. These were known as relics.

Our medieval ancestors believed that the saints inhabited the places where these relics resided. It made religion more popular because people felt they could get closer to the saints that way. I mean, if you think the shinbone of St Paul is lying in a box in your local parish church, you are more likely to get off your medieval backside and shuffle down to have a holy gawp at it. And if you were a bit shy of asking the Almighty for an extra loaf of bread because, quite reasonably, you thought He might have too much on his hands what with the plague and famine and endless Crusades between Christians and Infidels, blah blah, you could ask your saint of choice to step in and give you a helping hand.

Now some churchmen clearly believed that these relics were genuine but there were some – like the Pardoner in Chaucer's *Tales* – who knew they were on to a decent scam and would sell any old bits of bones that had fallen off the back of a dodgy medieval cart.

As Simon le Swindlemonger sets up his stall, a crowd of toothless, less than fragrant sinners gathers round: This is what I'll do for you. I've got letters from the Pope – a load of bulls* – going cheap. Guaranteed to give you a safe and painless passage to the Almighty. Bullus popus cheapus. I can't say fairer than that. And yes, madam, you're quite right, this bone here does look like a sheep's leg but is in fact the thigh bone of a seventh century saint who astounded the world on account of his unusual anatomy. Put this in your local drinking well and it will cure the diseases of all those who drink from it. Sheepus bonus curus scabus.

(*bulls were papal decrees)

The patron saint of medieval London was Erkenwald, a seventh-century monk. When he was an old and sick man he was carried through the city on a wooden cart. Not only was it thought that the remains of this old man would cure people of disease and disability but even fragments and splinters of the cart he was carried on were meant to have the same effect. This cart was enshrined behind the main altar of old St Paul's along with the remains of the monk, which were put into a lead casket in the shape of a church.

But London's most famous saint has to be Thomas à Becket, the London-born priest who became the Archbishop of Canterbury. The then King, Henry II, apparently said, 'Will no one rid me of this troublesome priest?' and a few knights who heard him sped off to Canterbury and hacked Thomas down at the altar of Canterbury Cathedral. This was in the twelfth century, but the cult of Thomas continued for at least another two hundred years. Londoners felt he was their special saint. The Chapel of St Thomas à Becket was built on London Bridge.

Chaucer's *Canterbury Tales* is about a motley crew of pilgrims setting off from a pub in Southwark – the Tabard – to Canterbury, to pay homage to St Thomas. No doubt the pilgrims would have gone in for a swift prayer before crossing to Southwark. With maybe – just maybe – a few swift pints at one of the taverns on the bridge. Here's a flavour of some of the characters in the poem, not exactly a very good advertisement for the Church:

The Nun wears very elegant clothes and beautiful jewellery, and knows all the right phrases and fashions from the French court.

The Summoner's job is to summon sinners to account for themselves at a holy court. He would do anything for money and is extremely spotty.

The Pardoner is the man who sells saints' bones and relics for holy pardons, i.e., if you've poisoned your neighbour's cat, then you can buy a rag off him and get a pardon into the bargain. He has scarily bulging eyes, limp yellow hair and admits that the piece of cloth he claims is the Virgin Mary's veil is, actually, a pillowcase.

The Monk loves horses and hunting.

The Friar plays the hurdy gurdy (a droning musical instrument, best not taken up), knows all the pubs in London and is very friendly with most of the barmaids who serve in them.

The most popular churchmen were the friars. This was because they were a bit more streetwise, and didn't mind getting their hands dirty. They were friendlier with the common people than the parsons and the priests, who mainly preached in Latin and even if you understood it, it was all about hellfire and brimstone. The friars were more like minstrels, they told stories that people liked and understood. All the monasteries had infirmaries as well, which were part of their building dedicated to curing the sick; they also had herb gardens to grow the ingredients for those mad medieval cures.

There were four 'orders' (types) of monks – the Dominicans, Franciscans, Carmelites and Austin Friars. They were 'mendicant' friars, which basically means they had to beg for their upkeep. While this wasn't exactly holding out their hands, begging on street corners, they did rely on charity given to them by Londoners – both poor and rich – to survive. Lots of rich people left the orders money in their wills.

The Blackfriars (Dominicans) were the first to get a London house, first in Holborn then between Ludgate and the Thames. King Edward I was their patron and the monastery became quite rich and in turn the friars provided a place where the king, Parliament, Chancery or King's Council could meet, and royal guests could stay.

Quite a contrast were the Greyfriars (Franciscans) who were given a house in Stinking Lane right by Newgate Shambles. There weren't many royal visitors popping their heads through these holy doors, although they were admired for their simple life and quite a few members of the royal family were buried here.

In 1349 one hundred friars died of the Black Death. Later one of history's most famous Londoners, Mayor Richard Whittington – you know the bloke with the cat – gave them money to build a library and £400-worth of books (a stonking amount of money in those days).

Many churches, priories and monasteries were set up through donations from the rich and high-born:

Henry I's wife Queen Matilda founded a leper hospital at St Giles-in-the-Fields

Henry I's former jester Rahere set up St Bartholomew's Hospital in Smithfield

King Stephen's wife founded St Katharine's near the Tower for female lepers

BILL THE BEARD BEATEN

ur Lionheart King – Richard I – has suppressed a rebellion that has threatened to overturn the safety of the nation. Some have been in sympathy with the uprising as it's said in some circles that the king is never here* and that he is always squeezing the city for funds, which he goes and spends in some far-flung part of the world.

But not us. We love him, honest. The rebellion was led by William Fitz-Osbert 'of the long beard', but his facial hair doesn't seem to have helped

in this situation. Bill the Beard sought sanctuary at St Mary-le-Bow in Cheap but the authorities hauled him out and hanged him at Smithfield along with eight others in front of his supporters.

(*Richard spent six months of his ten-year reign in England)

HOLY PIT STOPS

St. Pauls

St Paul's was the heart of London. Not only was it the main church of the city, it also attracted all levels of society. And the original spire was even higher than the dome we see today. Whereas we think of churches and churchyards as being peaceful havens, St Paul's was like a bustling market place, with all kinds of stalls set up in and around the church. There were even animals roaming around inside. In later centuries, during Shakespeare's day, St Paul's churchyard was the main place to buy books, but in the middle ages, before books were readily available, you were more likely to buy anything from food to services from a lawyer and to watch wrestling, hurling and leapfrog matches. Thieves of course also knew there were rich pickings to be had there.

St. Bartholomew's

This is the oldest hospital in London (though now on a different site). It was set up as a priory by the jester Rahere in 1123. Now why did he hang up his jester's hat and stripy tights to do this? He'd gone on a pilgrimage to Rome and caught malaria. During a fevered moment he had a vision of St Bartholomew, who said to him, 'Go home and found a hospital in my name' (saints do this) and that's exactly what he did. The hospital was staffed by a master, eight monks and four nuns who would go out into the streets and bring back the sick, orphaned, drunk and poor to look after them. Travellers could also get a bed for the night. As mentioned in an earlier chapter, Bartholomew Fair was intended originally to

raise money for the priory – and Rahere was known to get his juggling instruments out just for a day and relive his earlier career.

St. Giles-in-the-fields

St Giles was the patron saint of lepers and beggars so you can see why Queen Matilda set up the hospital here (roughly behind where Charing Cross Road and New Oxford Street meet). It was way out of the medieval city in an area that was at the time marshy fields, thought to be very unhealthy. She insisted that

as condemned prisoners walked from Newgate Prison to Tyburn to their place of execution, they would pass the door of St Giles and be given a 'cup of charity' before being hanged. St Giles became very famous in later centuries as a humble slum area, immortalized by the Victorian writer Charles Dickens.

Apart from (sometimes) offering succour to the poor and sick, London's churches also had another very important role: they provided sanctuary for people on the run from the law.

Top Tips for Timetravellers

1. If you've got a bit of a cold and the parish priest pops by unexpectedly, be very afraid

2. Old chicken bones do not guarantee a safe passage to heaven

3. Nor do old tights apparently worn by saints

4. Nor does a piece of wood that's fallen off an old cart

5. If it's a choice between hurdy gurdy and singing lessons, choose the latter – you'll keep more friends

CHAPTER SIX

CRIME AND PUNISHMENT

If you stepped out of line in medieval London there were all sorts of imaginative ways to punish you. Surprisingly they weren't that hot on torture, that came a bit later in our history, but they certainly made the punishment fit the crime.

There wasn't a police force as such in the city, but each ward was responsible for its own public safety – appointing beadles, bellmen, street keepers, constables and watchmen. The constable was the boss of the watchmen. Most crimes were inspired by drink and the work of the watchmen mainly involved locking up the drunks overnight until they appeared before the magistrate the next day.

Here are some medieval London by-laws

1. Strangers must not spend more than one day and one night in your house

2. Lepers are not allowed within the city walls

3. No one must walk out after the curfew

4. You may not wear a mask or false beard in public

5. If you are running a house of 'ill repute' you may have your windows and doors taken away

Most petty offenders were fined or imprisoned or subjected to public humiliation in a pillory (a wooden contraption where your hands and neck would be trapped, exposing you to the general public hurling anything at you from rotting vegetables to old fish and poo). He or she could be made to process through the streets, dragged on a hurdle or carried on horseback facing the tail and wearing a fool's cap, sometimes accompanied by a band of musicians – pipers and trumpeters.

He would literally be brought face to face with those he had defrauded, who were to chuck more or less anything at him. The prisoner would be made to do something symbolic of his crime, e.g.

A Baker would have rotten or underweight dough hung round his neck

A Taverner would be forced to drink his own sour wine for pretending to sell a better wine than was really on offer

A Butcher would be festooned with his own putrid meat

A Fraudster would have false coins or dice suspended around his neck

One man who defrauded people by selling them trinkets he said would cure their complaints was led through the city with one of the trinkets round his neck, plus a chamber pot hanging down his chest and another down his back.

Although these might not seem like extreme punishments, it meant that these people would never be trusted again and would most likely lose their livelihoods. Public ridicule was considered a powerful deterrent against other people committing similar crimes.

One condemned man was made to wear white shoes and a striped coat (think Laurence Llewelyn Bowen being made to wear a shell suit) with his head covered with a hood. The hangman rode behind him, carrying the rope in his hand, while his 'torturers' (people paid to publicly ridicule him) rode alongside mocking him from Chepe to Smithfield, his place of execution.

There were also specific times allocated in the pillory for different crimes:

- Spreading vicious reports about foreign traders – 1 hr

- Pretending to disguise base metal for silver – 1 hr

- Selling stale slices of eel – 1 hr

(Though I am tempted to say that the punishment for selling any slice of eel, fresh or stale, should be an hour...)

Q When do think they abolished the pillory?

Answer: 1837!

Punishments for assault:

For drawing a sword but not drawing blood
– half a mark or twelve days in Newgate

For drawing blood
– 20 shillings or forty days in Newgate

Striking with the fist, without bloodshed

– 2 shillings or eight days in Newgate (cheap at the price!)

Striking with the fist with bloodshed

– 40 pence or twelve days in Newgate

Murderers and thieves could be hanged, unless they could find refuge in one of London's one hundred and twenty churches or monasteries. The criminal could claim sanctuary for forty days and after that would be given a choice between surrendering for trial or forfeiting all his possessions, making for the nearest port and never returning to the country.

Although nearly everyone could claim sanctuary – murderers, debtors, thieves, even heretics – there were two exceptions: traitors and Jews (Londoners weren't very nice to Jews).

HENRY III FINALLY FORGIVES LONDON

Ever since Simon de Montfort and the King fell out, the relationship between the King and London has been very rocky. The King had been making himself unpopular with Londoners by favouring 'alien' tradesmen and taxing the city heavily. Simon de Montfort challenged his authority and was supported by London in a rebellion. However, this got out of hand when riots broke out – contributing to Londoners pelting Queen Eleanor in 1263.

The riots escalated when citizens started looting and pulling down houses. They attacked the Jews of the city, five hundred of whom died, and those who managed to escape sought sanctuary, along with the French and Italian merchants, at the Tower. De Montfort was finally defeated at the Battle of Evesham in Worcestershire in 1265, after which the King returned to punish the city, imposing huge fines and confiscating lands.

The King has recently announced his forgiveness, for which we are all very grateful.

One famous murderer, Miles Forrest, who is thought to have killed the two young nephews of Richard III in the Tower (at Richard's behest) was granted sanctuary at St Martin le Grand's, though he died there. This is one of the most famous murders in British history.

But there's no getting away from the fact, that most medieval murders in London at least were the result of silly arguments that got out of hand. It really was a recipe for disaster. Think about it: lots of drink about and – importantly – lots and lots of handy blunt instruments lying about the place. Here are just a few of the weapons available to your average Londoner:

Daggers and knives:
Irishnyf, Misericorde, Anelace, Fauchon, Traunchon, Poinard, Twytel, Baselard, Trenchour

Longer weapons:

Belte (type of axe), Poleax, Halberd, Sparth, Gysarme (two-edged blade), Bideu (blade a bit like a sickle)

Blunt instruments:
Talwhschide, Balstaf, Pikedstaff, Fagotstaff (pole for carrying wood), Durbarre, Wombedstaf, Bedstaff, Shovele.

You don't have to know what half of them are to get the picture – and that it's a shame that body armour wasn't compulsory for everyone at all times.

EDWARD I
ATTACKS JEWS
1290

The King has expelled 15,000 Jews from London. Their houses and synagogues have been taken over by Christians. It's thought that many have been massacred, though no one knows for sure the number. Some citizens who were against these attacks are already saying they can hear the cries of the victims at low tide at Gravesend. Those who were prepared to convert to Christianity have been allowed to stay. The Jews have been moneylenders to the citizens of London as it is forbidden for Christians to practise this under Church laws.

The King has been responding to certain pressure groups which are thought to have resented the wealth of the Jewish community. Many people are saying anonymously that this has been a grave mistake. Now Italians are being invited in to take the place of the Jewish citizens in their role as moneylenders.

The City is tense with speculation about how they will fare. Many people are talking again about a hundred years ago when in 1189, during the reign of Richard I (Lionheart), there was a terrible slaughter of the Jews, which writer Richard of Devizes called a 'holocaust'. This has not been London's finest hour.

True Medieval Crimes:

Extracts from Constable Pikehead's Casebook

The Case of the Bread Street Murders

In the year 1326 three servants of one Sir John Felton were delivering a horse to a man who lived in Bread Street. However the owner of the horse was ignorant of the fact. As they were proceeding down the street, they by chance met the owner of the horse who politely asked them to hand back the beast. This they refused to do. Taking some umbrage at this, the owner complained, whereupon one of the servants threatened him with a knife.

A passer-by noticed this altercation and decided to attack the knife-holder with his fists. At that point young John Felton, Sir John's son, by chance came out of a neighbouring house and with his sword in his hand attacked a man who had nothing to do with any of the above but who happened to be standing in a neighbouring doorway. Two other passers-by, noticing the growing fracas, joined the man who had previously used his fists and attacked young John Felton with pieces of wood, killing him. It is unclear whether the horse reached its intended destination.

The Case of the Horrible Husband

A couple went to sleep leaving a candle burning, which fell on the bed, setting it and the house alight. They were roused and managed to escape into the street. The husband decided it was his wife's fault and threw her back into the house, where she burnt to death.

The Case of the Arrant Earl of Arundel

In 1321 a squire of the Earl of Arundel was riding through Thames Street on his way to the Tower and nearly knocked over a woman carrying a child. A passer-by asked him politely to ride more carefully in the future and the squire felled him with his sword.

The Case of the Most Miserly Medieval Man

In the twelfth century John Overs was a ferryman across the Thames – basically a medieval London cabbie. Now while you'd think someone like this might not be the wealthiest man alive, through saving and lending people money [which meant that they would pay him huge amounts extra for the privilege when they paid him back] he was pretty rich. He was also rich because he was a wee bit miserly, a wee bit tight, you might say. So tight in fact that, because there was a custom in the Middle Ages that when a person died the household was not able to eat while there was a corpse in the house, he faked his own death to save some money on the food bill!

What he didn't take into account was that he wasn't terribly popular with his servants. On the news of his death they danced around his coffin joyfully, they sang and they stuffed their faces with food. John didn't like this and sat up. The servants, terrified he was a ghost, beat him to death. His only child, Marie, who lost her father not once but twice it now turned out, sent for her betrothed who, as he raced to her side, fell off his horse, broke his neck and died. Poor Marie decided to lead the holy life and set up a nunnery called St Mary Overie. And the moral of the tale is ... well ... don't try to come to your own funeral. There might be a little bit too much laughing and singing for comfort.

MURDER OF KING
SENDS NATION INTO SHOCK
1327

The nation is reeling with shock after news from Gloucestershire – that King Edward II has been murdered in the most unimaginably horrible way with a red-hot poker. It is being rumoured that Queen Isabella and her boyfriend Roger Mortimer are behind this savage regicide and that the King's fifteen-year-old son, who will become Edward III shortly, has been dragged into these dreadful events. Edward II has not been the most popular king, spending most of his time with pretty young men and doing DIY, particularly digging ditches and thatching, thought to be two of his favourite hobbies. Relations between the young Edward and his soon to-be-stepfather are said by insiders to be tense. *

(*When Edward III turned eighteen, he had Roger Mortimer executed.)

Most murders, if the criminal was unsuccessful in claiming sanctuary and escaping the country, were punishable by death – hanging, burning or beheading. The death penalty was always imposed on rebels and traitors or anyone who had threatened the king in any way or even touched something of the king's. A man was once hanged for touching the king's seal (his stamp of office)!

Once rebels and traitors had been executed, their heads would be boiled and stuck on London Bridge, perhaps with a crown of ivy, as a warning to others.

EXECUTION ROUND-UP

✦ 1305 ✦

Edward I's arch rival, the Scotsman William Wallace, has been hung, drawn and quartered in one of London's goriest executions to date at Smithfield. He was hanged until nearly dead, then cut down, after which his guts were cut out before his own eyes. After his beheading, his head was placed on the drawbridge of London Bridge, and can be viewed for the next few weeks. It is hoped that this will deter further rebellions.

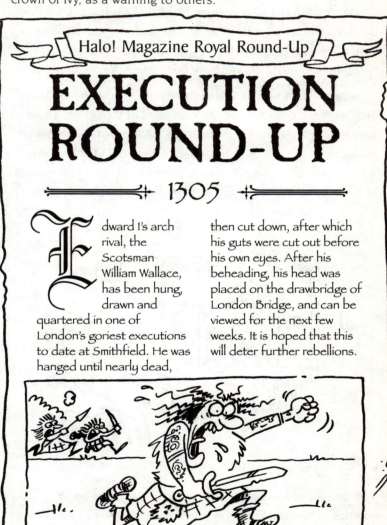

87

POISON PRISON

If you escaped the death penalty you might be thrown into prison. Built in the 12th century, Newgate Prison was probably London's worst hell-hole, although it has to be said there must have been a lot of competition. If you were destined for Newgate, you might as well have been given the death penalty.

One poor man who had been imprisoned because he was in debt for three shillings and sixpence died of starvation. There were always attempts by prisoners to escape. In 1419 sixty-four prisoners died of an epidemic of 'gaol fever'. In 1423 Richard Whittington left money in his will to ensure that Newgate could be rebuilt in a more civilized fashion. Unfortunately, it soon returned to its hellish conditions.

HOLY LOOPHOLE!

The 'benefit of the clergy' was one of those many, many oddities of medieval life. If you had been unable by every other means to squirm your way out of a death sentence for a crime you had committed you could recite a verse from the New

Testament. Your case would then be handed over to the Church, who would probably make you do a long stretch of penance (walking round saying how sorry you are and wearing uncomfortable clothes). But your life would be saved. Unsurprisingly, this became known as 'neck verse' as it saved your neck.

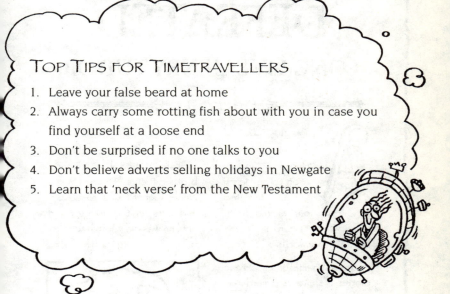

Top Tips for Timetravellers

1. Leave your false beard at home
2. Always carry some rotting fish about with you in case you find yourself at a loose end
3. Don't be surprised if no one talks to you
4. Don't believe adverts selling holidays in Newgate
5. Learn that 'neck verse' from the New Testament

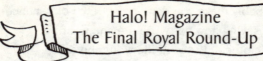
RICHARD III FINALLY
DEFEATED
– LONG LIVE HENRY TUDOR

1485

 fter two years of desperate turmoil, Henry Tudor, soon to be Henry VII, has defeated our wicked King, Richard III, at the Battle of Bosworth.

After a shameful career as plotter, deceiver and murderer, Richard put up a brave fight at the battle, even when he knew that he would be defeated. He finished a dishonourable life honourably.

Richard first came to power after his brother Edward IV died. It was hoped that Richard, then mere Duke of Gloucester, would take care

of his two young nephews – the next in line to the throne, Edward V and his younger brother, Richard Duke of York. Uncle Richard was to advise and counsel the young King until he was old enough to take full responsibility for his office.

But no sooner had Edward IV died than Richard marched the two young boys off to the Tower, telling them deceitfully that it was merely to prepare the young Edward for his coronation. As we are all too aware, this never happened and Richard seized the crown for himself. Housed in the Garden Tower, as it was then called, the boys were sometimes seen playing, but their public appearances became less and less frequent.

Although no one knows for sure the fate of these boys, it is widely thought that James Tyrell, a friend of King Richard III, arranged the boys' murder. The Garden Tower has now come to be known as the Bloody Tower...

It's time for us to bid farewell to those less than 'merrie' days of medieval London. Henry's victory over nasty Richard III began the Tudor age and that's another story.

(Editor's Note: To find out more why not read... The Timetraveller's Guide to Tudor London...)

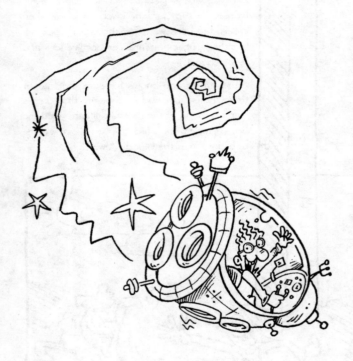

Places to Visit

Most of medieval London, thankfully, is long, long gone but there are still places where you can get a hint of what life would have been like in those plagued days.

The Museum of London, London Wall, EC2Y 5HN, is a great museum full of interesting exhibits about the history of London. The section on Medieval London is superb and has some great displays and artefacts – from Guild documents and a model of the Gothic St Paul's cathedral to pilgrims' badges and absurdly pointed medieval shoes. www.museumoflondon.org.uk. Tel 020 7600 3699.

Westminster Abbey, Westminster, SW1P 3PA. The buildings date from the Middle Ages and many of England's medieval monarchs, including Edward I and his beloved first wife Eleanor, are buried here. You can also visit Geoffrey Chaucer, author of *The Canterbury Tales*, the first poet to be laid to rest in Poets' Corner. www.westminster-abbey.org. Tel 020 7222 5152.

The Guildhall, Guildhall Yard, EC2P 2EJ, was built in 1411 and has survived both the Great Fire of London in 1666 and the Blitz of the Second World War. Freedom of the City ceremonies, like those for the medieval apprentices, are still held here. Outside the marvellous Guildhall Art Gallery nearby, there's also a statue of the great Mayor of London Dick Whittington and his cat! www.corpoflondon.gov.uk. Tel 020 7606 3030.

St Michael Paternoster, Royal College Hill off Thames Street, was Dick Whittington's church – he lived next door and was buried here. His grave was lost in the Great Fire of London in 1666 but a stained glass window commemorates his deeds.

The Museum of the Order of St John, St John's Gate, St John's Lane, Clerkenwell, London EC1 4DA, traces the history of the courtly, crusading knights the Hospitallers. There's a twelfth-century crypt and you can view books dating from the thirteenth century, along with arms and armour, paintings and booty the knights brought back from Malta.

Old Jewry, Cheapside, EC2, was the former home of London's Jewish community and here you will find a plaque which marks the site of the Great Synagogue which stood here until 1272. At Ironmonger's Lane, Cheapside, EC2, just down the road from Old Jewry there's another plaque, this one records the birthplace of the murdered archbishop Thomas à Beckett.

St Magnus the Martyr, Lower Thames Street, EC3R 6DN, once stood at the head of London Bridge. The church was rebuilt after the Great Fire of London but just inside there's a brilliant model of Old London Bridge. If you look carefully by the gate as you enter you can also spot stones from the bridge.

St Bride's, Bride's Lane off Fleet Street, EC4, like St Magnus was also rebuilt after the Great Fire but its crypt is ancient, spooky and worth a look. The unpopular King John held his parliament at St Bride's in 1210.

St Giles Cripplegate, Fore Street, EC2, is one of the oldest churches in the City, with a tower that dates from the Middle Ages. Queen Matilda originally established a house for lepers here in 1090.

The London Dungeon, 28–34 Tooley Street, London Bridge, SE1 2SZ, is London's top spot for terrifying medieval tortures and disgusting dungeons. Not for the faint-hearted but fun. www.thedungeons.com. Tel 020 7403 7221.

The Old Operating Theatre, Museum and Herb Garrett, 9a St Thomas Street, London SE1 9RY, gives an insight into grisly medicinal techniques such as those practised by the barber-surgeons. www.thegarret.org.uk. Tel 020 7955 4791.

The British Museum, Great Russell Street, Bloomsbury, WC1B 3DG, has an array of medieval objects, particularly pottery. Most aren't directly connected with London, but they give some idea of how medieval people lived. www.thebritishmuseum.ac.uk. Tel 020 7636 1555.

OTHER BOOKS FROM WATLING STREET YOU'LL LOVE
IN THIS SERIES:

The Timetraveller's Guide to Roman London
by Olivia Goodrich
Find out just why Rome's craziest emperors invaded cool, cruel Britannia
and built a city besides the Thames.
ISBN 1-904153-06-2

•

The Timetraveller's Guide to Saxon and Viking London
by Joshua Doder
Journey back to London when it was home to some of the funniest
names and the foulest food in English history!
ISBN 1-904153-07-0

•

The Timetraveller's Guide to Shakespeare's London
by Joshua Doder
William Shakespeare is our greatest writer; read all about him, his plays
and the big bad city he lived and worked in.
ISBN 1-904153-10-0

•

The Timetraveller's Guide to Tudor London
by Natasha Narayan
See the terrible tyrants, cruel queens, con men and cutpurses in Tudor
London's dark, dingy and all too dangerous streets.
ISBN 1-904153-09-7

•

The Timetraveller's Guide to Victorian London
by Natasha Narayan
Get robbed and meet the snobs on a tour of Queen Vic's top town.
ISBN 1-904153-11-9

In case you have difficulty finding any Watling St books in your local
bookshop, you can place orders directly through

BOOKPOST,
Freepost, PO Box 29, Douglas, Isle of Man IM99 1BQ

Telephone 01634 836000
email: bookshop@enterprise.net